Also by Jaroslaw Jankowski

Why Are We So Different?
Your Guide to the 16 Personality Types

Why are we so very different from one another?
Why do we organise our lives in such disparate
ways? Why are our modes of assimilating
information so varied? Why are our approaches to
decision-making so diverse? Why are our forms of
relaxing and 'recharging our batteries' so dissimilar?

Your Guide to the 16 Personality Types will help you to
understand both yourselves and other people better.
It will aid you not only in avoiding any number of
traps, but also in making the most of your personal
potential, as well as in taking the right decisions
about your education and career and in building
healthy relationships with others.
The book contains the ID16™© Personality
Test, which will enable you to determine your own
personality type. It also offers a comprehensive
description of each of the sixteen types.

The Presenter

Your Guide
to the ESFP Personality Type

The ID16™© Personality Types series

JAROSLAW JANKOWSKI
M.Ed., EMBA

LOGOS
MEDIA

This is a book which can help you exploit your potential more fully, build healthy relationships with other people and make the right decisions about your education and career. However, it should not be considered to be a substitute for expert physiological or psychiatric consultation. Neither the author nor the publisher accept any responsibility whatsoever for any detrimental effects which may result from the inappropriate use of this book.

ID16™© is an independent typology developed by Polish educator and manager Jaroslaw Jankowski and grounded in Carl Gustav Jung's theory. It should not be confused with the personality typologies and tests proposed by other authors or offered by other institutions.

Original title: Twój typ osobowości: Prezenter (ESFP)
Translated from the Polish by Caryl Swift
Proof reading: Lacrosse | experts in translation
Layout editing by Zbigniew Szalbot

Published by LOGOS MEDIA

Paperback: ISBN 978-83-7981-087-1
EPUB: ISBN 978-83-7981-088-8
MOBI: ISBN 978-83-7981-089-5

Contents

Preface

The work in your hands is a compendium of knowledge on the *presenter*. It forms part of the *ID16™© Personality Types* series, which consists of sixteen books on the individual personality types and *Who Are You? The ID16™© Personality Test*, an introduction to the ID16™© independent personality typology, which is based on the theory developed by Carl Gustav Jung.

As you explore this book on the *presenter*, you will find the answer to a number of crucial questions:

- How do *presenters* think and what do they feel? How do they make decisions? How do they solve problems? What makes them anxious? What do they fear? What irritates them?
- Which personality types are they happy to encounter on their road through life and which ones do they avoid? What kind of

friends, life partners and parents do they make? How do others perceive them?

- What are their vocational predispositions? What sort of work environment allows them to function most effectively? Which careers best suit their personality type?
- What are their strengths and what do they need to work on? How can they make the most of their potential and avoid pitfalls?
- Which famous people correspond to the *presenter*'s profile?

The book also contains the most essential information about the ID16™© typology.

We sincerely hope that it will help you in coming to know yourself and others better.

ID16™© and Jungian Personality Typology

ID16™© numbers among what are referred to as Jungian personality typologies, which draw on the theories developed by Carl Gustav Jung (1875-1961), a Swiss psychiatrist and psychologist and a pioneer of the 'depth psychology' approach.

On the basis of many years of research and observation, Jung came to the conclusion that the differences in people's attitudes and preferences are far from random. He developed a concept which is highly familiar to us today: the division of people into extroverts and introverts. In addition, he distinguished four personality functions, which form two opposing pairs: sensing-intuition and thinking-feeling. He also established that one function is dominant in each pair. He became convinced that each and every person's dominant functions are fixed and independent of external conditions and that, together, what they form is a personality type.

In 1938, two American psychiatrists, Horace Gray and Joseph Wheelwright, created the first personality test based on Jung's theories. It was designed to make it possible to determine the dominant functions within the three dimensions described by Jung, namely, **extraversion-introversion**, **sensing-intuition** and **thinking-feeling**. That first test became the inspiration for other researchers. In 1942, again in America, Isabel Briggs Myers and Katherine Briggs began using their own personality test, broadening Gray's and Wheelwright's classic, three-dimensional model to include a fourth: **judging-perceiving**. The majority of subsequent personality typologies and tests drawing on Jung's theories also take that fourth dimension into account. They include the American typology published by David W. Keirsey in 1978 and the personality test developed in the nineteen seventies by Aušra Augustinavičiūtė, a Lithuanian psychologist. Over the following decades, other European researchers followed in their footsteps, creating more four-dimensional personality typologies and tests for use in personal coaching and career counselling.

ID16™© figures among that group. An independent typology developed by Polish educator and manager Jaroslaw Jankowski, it was published in the first decade of the twenty-first century. ID16™© is based on Carl Jung's classic theory and, like other contemporary Jungian typologies, it follows a four-dimensional path, terming those dimensions the **four natural inclinations**. These inclinations are dichotomous in nature and the picture they provide gives us information regarding a person's personality type. Analysis of the first inclination is intended to determine the dominant **source of life energy**, this being either the exterior or the interior world. Analysis of the second inclination defines the dominant **mode of assimilating information**, which occurs via the senses or via intuition. Analysis of the third inclination supplies a description of the **decision-making mode**, where either mind or heart is dominant, while analysis of the fourth inclination produces a definition of the dominant **lifestyle** as either organised or spontaneous. The combination of all these natural inclinations results in **sixteen possible personality types**.

One remarkable feature of the ID16™© typology is its practical dimension. It describes the individual personality types in action – at work, in daily life and in interpersonal relations. It neither concentrates on the internal dynamics of personality nor does it undertake any theoretical attempts at explaining or commenting on invisible, interior processes. The focus is turned more toward the ways in which a given personality type manifests itself externally and how it affects the surrounding world. This emphasis on the social aspect of personality places ID16™© somewhat closer to the previously mentioned typology developed by Aušra Augustinavičiūtė.

Each of the ID16™© personality types is the result of a given person's natural inclinations. There is nothing evaluative or judgemental about ascribing a person to a given type, though. No particular personality type is 'better' or 'worse' than any other. Each type is quite simply different and each has its own potential strengths and weaknesses. ID16™© makes it possible to identify and describe those differences. It helps us to understand ourselves and discover our place in the world.

Familiarity with our personality profile enables us to make full use of our potential and work on the areas which might cause us trouble. It is an invaluable aid in everyday life, in solving problems, in building healthy relationships with other people and in making decisions relating to our education and careers.

Determining personality is a process which is neither arbitrary nor mechanical in nature. As the 'owner and user' of our personality, each and every one of us is fully capable of defining which type we belong to. The individual's role is thus pivotal. This self-identification can be achieved either by analysing the descriptions of the ID16™© personality types and steadily narrowing down the fields of choice or by taking the short cut provided by the ID16™© Personality Test.[1] The role played by each 'personality user' is equally crucial when it comes to the test, given that the outcome depends entirely on the answers they provide.

Identifying personality types helps us to know both ourselves and others. Nonetheless, it should not be treated as some kind of future-determining oracle. No personality type can ever justify our weaknesses or poor interpersonal relationships. It might, however, help us to understand their causes!

ID16™© treats personality type not as a static, genetic, pre-determined condition, but as a product

---

[1] The test can be found in *Why Are We So Different? Your Guide to the 16 Personality Types* by Jaroslaw Jankowski.

of innate and acquired characteristics. As such, it is a concept which neither diminishes free will nor engages in pigeonholing people. What it does is open up new perspectives for us, encouraging us to work on ourselves and indicating the areas where that work is most needed.

The Presenter (ESFP)

The Personality in a Nutshell

Life motto: Now is the perfect moment!

In brief, *presenters* …

are optimistic, energetic and outgoing, with the ability to enjoy life and have fun to the full. Practical, flexible and spontaneous at one and the same time, they enjoy change and new experiences, coping badly with solitude, stagnation and routine.

With their liking for being at the centre of attention, they are natural-born actors and their speaking abilities arouse the interest and enthusiasm of their listeners. Focused as they are on the present moment, they will sometimes lose sight of their long-term aims and can also have problems with foreseeing the consequences of their actions.

The *presenter's* four natural inclinations:

- source of life energy: the exterior world
- mode of assimilating information: via the senses
- decision-making mode: the heart
- lifestyle: spontaneous

Similar personality types:

- the Advocate
- the Artist
- the Protector

Statistical data:

- *presenters* constitute between eight and thirteen per cent of the global community
- women predominate among *presenters* (60 per cent)
- Brazil is an example of a nation corresponding to the *presenter's* profile[2]

The Four-Letter Code

In terms of Jungian personality typology, the universal four-letter code for the *presenter* is ESFP.

---

[2] What this means is not that all the residents of Brazil fall within this personality type, but that Brazilian society as a whole possesses a great many of the character traits typical of the *presenter*.

General character traits

Presenters are extraordinarily optimistic and spontaneous, with an ability to enjoy every moment and a driving urge to make the most of life. When they do something, they commit themselves to it with every ounce of their energy. They love change, new experiences and surprises, and will always gravitate towards the action, wherever it might be.

As others see them

Presenters like people and know how to gain genuine pleasure from any and every get-together and conversation. Concern for others and their love of shared fun lie at the heart of their interpersonal relationships, while their optimism, openness and ability to enjoy life arouse other people's admiration and quite often cause them to start taking a more positive view of the world.

Usually brimming with energy, they are the life and soul of any gathering – wherever they appear, their behaviour makes them the focus of attention and other people will always have a wonderful time and forget their problems in their company. Indeed, they will sometimes have the impression that they are taking part in some kind of performance, since *presenters* are not only natural-born actors, but also have a superb sense of humour. Capable of commenting on reality and talking about their own myriad adventures and vicissitudes in a strikingly colourful way, they are perfectly capable of holding forth for hours when they have an audience, introducing a diverse range of subplots and a host of digressions along the way. Even when their listeners are well aware of their tendency to heighten and embroider the facts, they still hear them out with bated breath ... and will often also be struck with envy for their fascinating lives and the ability to take delight in every day.

Presenters themselves gain an enormous sense of satisfaction from the fact that they can infuse others with optimism and help them to have fun or inspire them to act. If they are involved in a gathering, they will frequently take on the role of compère or master of ceremonies and are absolutely in their element when introducing the programme and presenting the people taking part ... hence the name for this personality type.

With the sincere interest, acceptance and liking they feel for others, the majority of their relationships are excellent. However, some people are irritated by their carefree, nonchalant style and by the fact that they bend their efforts to focus attention on themselves and continually expect recognition and acceptance. Others accuse them of being superficial, irresponsible and incapable of reflecting more profoundly on life.

As the reverse side of that coin, people who take life too seriously set *presenters'* teeth on edge and they are infuriated by passivity, pessimism, faint enthusiasm and apathy, while any incidence of giving efficiency and profit priority over human happiness acts on them like a red rag to a bull. They also have difficulty in understanding loners who live in a world of their own and are engrossed in abstract theories or philosophical delvings. Indeed, they themselves find long-term solitude extremely hard to bear: no *presenter* has it in them to become a hermit!

Amongst others

Presenters are a bottomless well of fresh news, up-to-the-minute information and the latest jokes – so much so that many another person wonders where and how on earth they manage to get hold of it all. In general, they also know how other people are doing and what they are up to. However, this is not in the least because they have a leaning towards gossip; what it springs from is their genuine interest in people, their ability to put themselves in their shoes and the fact that they are both excellent listeners and skilled observers of human behaviour. In short, they make outstanding confidants and confidantes and other people sense this and are thus happy to share their experiences with them. Talking to a *presenter* leaves people heartened and inspired, helped by the awareness that someone has listened to them attentively, understood what they have been going through and given voice to what they themselves are feeling.

As a rule, they will make the most of any and every chance to get together with people and have a good time with them. They almost never give a family celebration or social gathering a miss and tend to seize every opportunity for making merry, be it a birthday, a name day, an anniversary or any and every other kind of 'high day and holiday', and are just as delighted to organise such events themselves, including lavish parties to mark more significant occasions. Even when they are snowed under with work, they manage to find the time to drop in on their friends. By the same token, unexpected visits will also always give them joy.

As *presenters* see it, the here and now matters more than the future and people are more important than work, duties and obligations. Relinquishing their pleasures and the opportunity to enjoy themselves thus comes very hard to them. Indeed, they love entertainment and having fun so much that it will sometimes become an end in itself for them and, in their pursuit of pleasure, new experiences and experiment, they may well shed all boundaries and inhibitions. In fact, their inclination to take risks can sometimes lead not only to their exposing themselves to danger, but even to ruining their health or to their descent into addiction.

Attitudes

Presenters set tremendous store by both their own freedom and independence and that of others. As such, they are highly sensitive to any manifestation of constraint in that respect. Exhibiting zero tolerance when it comes to attempts to exercise excessive control over people, standardise them, pigeonhole them or treat them like cogs in a machine, they themselves respect other people's individualism and believe that every person has their own, unique value and is irreplaceable.

By nature wholly uninterested in abstract theories and concepts which cannot be transferred directly into life as it is being lived in the present, they would rather move through a world of concrete data and tangible facts. Deliberating on hypothetical possibilities and potential opportunities, hazards or threats is a form of torture to them and it is rare indeed for them to spend time envisioning long-term plans for the future.

This aversion to planning means that they would rather wait and see what each day brings and respond there and then, depending on how things develop.

They live life in the immediate present, endeavouring to make the most of what today offers and rarely indulging in memories of the past or cogitating about the future. For instance, given their focus on the present moment, the notion of 'putting something away for a rainy day' or 'saving for retirement' is alien to their mindset: if *presenters* have some spare funds, they would rather put them to use here and now. In their book, time spent worrying over what tomorrow may bring is time wasted. Better to relish the moment and deal with problems as and when they occur and, since they are highly flexible and endowed with superb improvisational skills, they are well equipped to do so, coping well in rapidly shifting circumstances which demand immediate reaction to fresh factors and lightning-fast adaptation to new situations.

Perception and thinking

Presenters have a developed aesthetic sense and spatial imagination, along with a natural artistic talent. With their finger on the pulse as far as 'trending now … what's in and what's out' is concerned, they are often interested in the fashion scene. Their homes are distinctive for their style and they have the ability to furnish and decorate them in a way which endows the space with a warm cosiness. They display greater culinary skills than most, an aspect of their nature which goes hand in hand with their love of good food.

Learning most readily through observation, experimentation and experience, *presenters* are pragmatic by nature, with an interest in what they can touch, experience or taste. They enjoy practical tasks and are happy to help other people solve concrete, tangible problems, sparing neither time nor energy in their efforts. When they run into a complex issue or complicated situation, they will do everything within their power to simplify things. At the same time, however, they have a tendency to trivialise matters and the solutions they proffer can thus be inadequate and makeshift in that they avert the problem or get rid of it temporarily, but fail to root it out once and for all.

Presenters dislike situations which are difficult, ambivalent or anything less than limpidly transparent. Their image of the world is usually black and white, so any contact with the fuzziness of a reality where white is not entirely white and black is not wholly black causes them an immense sense of unease. Their reaction is often to retreat into simplification, whereby they will whitewash the 'white' to bleached perfection or densify the 'black' to the darkest of depths.

Decisions

When *presenters* have to make a decision, they will consider its impact on other people and frequently both consult their friends and acquaintances and reach for the opinions of those around them. They are generally guided by common sense and, distrusting intuition and presentiments, they base their thinking on facts and hard data. On the whole, being capable of assessing a situation and the existing possibilities rapidly, they are not inclined to spend overmuch time on analysing all the pros and cons, but tend to avail themselves of their lightning-fast ability to select what they deem to be the best and most sensible solution. This means that they normally make decisions fairly quickly.

Presenters fare best when it comes to current and immediate issues relating to concrete and tangible problems. On the other hand, they face the greatest difficulty when confronted with the need to make decisions which require them to foresee long-term consequences, turn their thoughts to the future and take into consideration factors which have not yet occurred, such as potential threats or hazards that may crop up at a more distant moment.

Enthusiasms

Presenters are attracted by anything fresh and original, be it new friends and acquaintances, new ideas, new products, new experiences, new fashions – the list is endless! They are usually familiar with the latest trends, innovations and novelties and will often be the first in their circle to know about newly opened restaurants, clubs or pubs, upcoming events and concerts and the latest products and offers on the market.

They revel in the fact that every day may bring something new and every moment might have a surprise in store. This, of course, means that they suffer when life turns monotonous and boring, offering them nothing but routine and stagnation. Nonetheless, they are capable of finding something exciting in every situation and normally make an effort to introduce some element of fun and appeal into any job they are doing in order to be able to extract some kind of pleasure from it.

Communication

Talking to other people gives *presenters* enormous pleasure and they are unrestrained when it comes to adding their voice to a group. Natural-born speakers, compères and presenters, their presence introduces a warm, friendly atmosphere and they are more than capable of keeping their audience entertained. They have no fear of appearing in public and their affinity for the spotlight is inbuilt. When they lead a presentation or announce a public appearance, they make full use of their acting abilities, gift for improvisation and sense of humour.

They have the ability to fire their listeners with enthusiasm, influence the way they see the world and spur them into action. Called upon to explain a task, goal or initiative, they do so in a way which is both utterly natural and uncommonly appealing. Their usual style is extremely clear, precise, down-to-earth and direct. On the other hand, they dislike expressing their thoughts in writing and most definitely favour verbal communication and person-to-person contact.

With their superb interpersonal skills and gift of empathy, they are able both to 'read' people and spot their hidden motives and problems. However, voicing critical opinions and calling other people's attention to inappropriate behaviour, for instance, is something they find tough to deal with. In turn, they themselves can scarcely bear criticism levelled at them by others; they struggle to apply it constructively and often perceive it as an act of spitefulness or as an attack on them or an attempt to undermine their values. When that happens, they are capable of reacting strongly in their own defence and may well end up saying things they will later regret.

In the face of stress

Tasks requiring lengthy concentration, deep reflection, working independently or long-term, strategic planning will usually trigger tension and a sense of anxiety in *presenters*. Under the influence of lasting stress, they may well start constructing black scenarios in their thoughts or seek relief from the tension by turning to sensual pleasures or substances. Fortunately, though, they do also have the ability to relax more constructively, pursuing various sporting activities or organising parties, picnics and family outings in order to spend time with their friends, acquaintances and nearest and dearest. If one thing is certain, it is the fact that they will never number amongst those whose idea of a perfect break is immersing themselves in a good book or solving brain-teasers!

Socially

Presenters are extremely outgoing and highly approachable. They treat everyone as if they were old friends and people who are meeting them for the first time will often have the impression that they have known them for ages. 'Direct', 'uncomplicated' and 'flexible to the max' are all descriptions which fit *presenters* like a glove!

People are a highly important aspect of their lives. Caring for others gives them tremendous joy and, when a helping hand is held out to them, they are equally as capable of availing themselves of it. With an eye always firmly fixed on a pleasant atmosphere and warm interpersonal relations, they find situations of conflict almost impossible to bear and will do anything to prevent them from arising. By the same token, their efforts to avoid disagreeable conversations often trigger their inclination to sweep a problem under the carpet or pretend that it is non-existent.

Amongst friends

In the main, *presenters* are extremely open, outgoing and ready to strike up new acquaintanceships. With their ability to 'read' people on the spot, they will often know exactly who they are dealing with after no more than a few minutes of conversation with someone. Warm, friendly relationships with others are one of the most important things in their lives and, with their genuine desire for people's happiness, they are unstinting with their time, energy and money when it comes to helping them or, quite simply, to whiling away the time pleasantly in their company. They find solitude hard to bear, but it is their good fortune to be surrounded by people most of the time, since their optimism, sense of humour, warmth, empathy and sincerity act like a magnet to others. People quite simply enjoy their company and are happy to share their experiences and problems with them; and the trust and sympathy of others is a source of happiness and satisfaction to *presenters* themselves.

Other people's opinions count for a great deal with *presenters* and they are open to the influence of their surroundings. However, although they are able to adapt to the current situation and take the needs of others into consideration, they will not allow themselves to be used. In general, their friends and acquaintances are legion, but the majority of these relationships are fairly superficial in nature. They are given to devoting most of their attention to new relationships and neglecting those which have existed for some time. They tend to have no more than a handful of close friends, who are most often *advocates*, *artists*, *enthusiasts* or other *presenters* and, most rarely, *strategists*, *directors* and *logicians*.

As life partners

As a partner for life, *presenters* bring warmth, energy and optimism to the relationship. For the person by their side, boredom is simply not an option, since they make it their personal business to ensure that something is always going on and provide their partner with all kinds of attractions. Within the microcosm of their family, the *presenter* usually takes on the office of 'foreign minister', assuming responsibility for its contact with the wider world and acting as its representative there. As a rule, they set great store by birthdays, anniversaries and every other kind of family celebration, and not only love organising get-togethers of all sorts but will also gleefully step into the role of master of ceremonies if given half a chance. They spare neither time nor money on arranging such events, an attitude perceived by some as a sign of extravagance. Indeed, given that their partners will often see other, more pressing needs, while *presenters* themselves can think of almost nothing which takes priority over enjoying a celebration with family and friends, this tendency can sometimes lead to tension within their relationship.

The fact is that *presenters* are, by nature, extremely generous; they neither calculate nor are they niggardly in the least. Their love is unconditional; they give of themselves unstintingly and expect nothing in return. Their feelings are deep, fervent and sensual and their partner's happiness is their dearest wish. They do all they can to meet their needs, showing them enormous warmth and unrestrainedly offering them tender words and affectionate gestures. They, too, need warmth, closeness and acceptance. Given that they are profoundly affected by any kind of cutting remark or unflattering comment, they are easily hurt and they tend not only to treat criticism of their actions as a personal attack, but also to respond with a counter-attack.

However, discussing tough and unpleasant issues is anathema to *presenters* and they will try to avoid conflicts and arguments at any price. They also face problems coping with long-term obligations and, since their nature is to live for today rather than turn their thoughts to the future, swearing constancy "until death do us part" will normally demand enormous commitment on their part. At the same time, their need for new experiences, their inclination to experiment, their leaning towards risk-taking and their love of sensual pleasures can pose a threat to the stability of their relationships

The natural candidates for a *presenter's* life partner are people of a personality type akin to their own: *advocates, artists* or *protectors*. Building mutual understanding and harmonious relations will be easier in a union of that kind. Nonetheless, experience has taught us that people are also capable of creating happy and successful relationships despite what would seem to be an evident typological incompatibility. Moreover, the differences between two partners can lend added dynamics to a relationship and engender personal development. Indeed, for many people, this is a prospect that appears more attractive than the vision of a harmonious relationship wherein concord and full, mutual understanding hold sway.

As parents

Presenters make extremely caring parents who show their children great warmth and have the ability to see the world through their eyes, a skill which means that they know what will bring them the most joy. They provide a host of attractions, arranging happy surprises and celebrating their successes with enormous pride, which is tremendously encouraging and motivating. They love spending time with their offspring, having fun with them and talking to them. In general, hubbub and commotion leaves them completely unperturbed; when the children are enjoying themselves, their *presenter* parents are happy. Practical parenting tasks come easily to them and parental responsibilities hold no fears for them. They encourage their offspring to be themselves, live out their own dreams and make the most of their own strengths.

As a rule, they are not overly demanding and struggle to put discipline into practice, especially since they themselves are often not entirely convinced as to its point. As a result, their children sometimes have problems in distinguishing good and desirable behaviour from that which is bad and reprehensible. *Presenter*s usually prefer partnership parenting and, in the main, they are tolerant, uncomplicated and understanding. However, they can sometimes be strict and impatient, since their approach frequently lacks cohesion and consistency. If the other parent is unable to operate in a more organised fashion, their children might lack a sense of security and stability, as well as clear rules telling them how the world is run.

As adults, their children usually recall their *presenter* parents as warm, caring and sincere. They have fond memories of the countless unforgettable attractions they provided and of the way that they offered them a great deal of freedom, encouraged them to fulfil their dreams and gave them unconditional support during tough moments.

Work and career paths

Motion, variety and change are meat and drink to *presenters*, who are attracted to work which offers possibilities for being creative, experimenting and solving concrete, tangible and practical problems.

Companies and institutions

Presenters are happiest working for organisations with a non-linear structure, where the staff are given considerable freedom of action and a say in decisions affecting them. They enjoy being wherever things are going on and find bureaucracy, hierarchies, routine, repetitive tasks and rigid procedures unbearable, while writing up accounts of their activities, preparing reports and compiling data are tasks which they consider tiresome in the extreme. They also have no liking for working individually. However, they excel when it comes to work demanding interpersonal skills, inventiveness, flexibility and the ability to improvise. They fit in well in institutions geared towards the good of society and bringing about tangible and positive changes in the life of the local community or the country or on a global scale.

Tasks

Presenters will throw themselves wholeheartedly into accomplishing tasks they believe in. They like knowing that their activities have a positive impact on other people's lives and help them to solve their problems, and they are usually greatly concerned to ensure that their colleagues, clients and those under their care are satisfied.

In general, they dislike work of a conceptual nature and are at a particular loss when they are unable either to refer to similar experiences from the past or count on pointers from someone else. Concentrating and focusing on tasks requiring long-term commitment is also something they often find challenging, especially when the results of their work are a distant prospect or the aim of the job is less than crystal clear. They are easily distracted and, in the battle for their attention, it is usually the newest and most powerful stimulus which will emerge victorious. Once a new, more exciting project appears on the horizon, they will struggle to continue with what they have already begun. They are happiest when engaged on short-term jobs and are capable multitaskers.

As part of a team

When working as part of a team, *presenters* are uncomplicated and flexible members who value a healthy and friendly atmosphere and take care to ensure that no one feels passed over or excluded. It is absolutely normal for them to forge strong bonds with their colleagues and just as rare for them to give a social gathering or integration event a miss.

Given that they themselves make every effort to avoid conflicts and disputes, they find people who set out on the path to confrontation, fight to win power and authority and are capable of hurting their colleagues wholly incomprehensible. However, their own readiness to do all they can to meet the needs of others and make their jobs easier means that they are skilled at building compromises and what very often happens is that they naturally emerge as the group's representative, acting as its spokesperson and presenting its position to a wider audience.

Views on workplace hierarchy

Presenters prefer superiors who see those they are in charge of as people and not as tools serving to accomplish a goal. They like their bosses to be flexible, open to innovative solutions and ready to point their subordinates in the general direction they should take, while affording them freedom in accomplishing their tasks and respecting their individual style of working.

When they themselves take on the responsibility of leading others, they adopt a similar approach, valuing their relationships with those in their charge and never failing to put people before results and achievements. However, when they hold a management position, their overly lenient attitude and inability to discipline the weaker members of their team frequently poses a problem.

Professions

Knowledge of our own personality profile and natural preferences provides us with invaluable help in choosing the optimal path in our professional careers. Experience has shown that, while *presenters* are perfectly able to work and find fulfilment in a range of fields, their personality type naturally predisposes them to the following fields and professions:

- acting
- advisor
- carer
- consultant
- entrepreneur
- events organiser
- fashion designer
- florist
- human resources
- insurance agent
- interior designer
- leisure and recreation centres
- lifeguard
- musician
- paramedic
- life coach
- photographer
- psychologist
- physician
- public relations
- radio or television presenter
- receptionist
- sales representative
- social welfare
- sports trainer
- stylist
- teacher
- therapist
- travel agent

- visual artist
- vet

Potential strengths and weaknesses

Like any other personality type, *presenters* have their potential strengths and weaknesses and this potential can be cultivated in a variety of ways. *Presenters'* personal happiness and professional fulfilment depend on whether they make the most of the 'pluses' offered by their personality type and face up to its inherent dangers. Here, then, is a SUMMARY of those 'pluses' and dangers:

Potential strengths

Presenters are enthusiastic, spontaneous and flexible. Capable of reacting rapidly to shifting circumstances and adapting to new conditions, they are practical and learn fast. With their love of experiment and fearless attitude towards risk, they cope well with change and, being optimistic by nature, they are not disheartened by obstacles and difficulties. They also have the ability to enjoy every day and make the most of every moment. Their enthusiasm and optimism is infectious and tends to have a positive impact on others and, when they work as part of a group, they are able both to integrate the team and build comprises. Their interest in other people and concern for their happiness and well-being is genuine, as is their respect for their freedom and individuality. They are always ready to lend a helping hand and, at one and the same time, have no trouble in either accepting assistance from others or in making the most of their experience and advice.

Excellent observers of the world around them and of human emotions and feelings, they are just as skilled at rapidly 'reading' other people. With their outgoing, open nature, they are easy to get to know and, in general, they are sought-after companions. Their optimism and sense of humour draws others to them, while their warm, sincere interest encourages people to confide in them. Their inherent acting skills go hand in hand with a developed artistic and aesthetic sense, and they are natural-born speakers, compères and presenters, endowed with the ability to arouse the interest and enthusiasm of their listeners. Remarkably generous and ready to meet the needs of others, they love not only helping them, but also giving them gifts, offering them a variety of attractions, preparing surprises for them and finding ways for them to while away the time pleasantly – all of which is helped by their ability to adapt to whatever the circumstances may currently be.

Potential weaknesses

Presenters face an uphill struggle when it comes to extending their thoughts beyond the here and now, carrying out jobs which demand that they envisage what may happen in the future or sacrifice current pleasures for the sake of distant benefits. Tasks which require lengthy focus and concentration or require them to work alone are a source of misery to them, particularly when the outcome of their efforts will only become visible with time. They also view the world of abstract concepts and complex theories as unmapped and impenetrable territory and are inclined both to ignore anything which cannot be turned into practical action and to over-simplify, or quite often, even to trivialise problems. To *presenters*, the ideal solution will always be one which is straightforward, fast and requires nothing much in the way of penetrating reflection. While this approach enables them to get rid of a problem that has arisen – and thus turn their energies to more pleasant pursuits – it rarely affords them an understanding of the underlying causes. By the same token, their focus on fun, pleasure and entertainment means that they sometimes fail to discern life's more profound dimensions.

Understanding diverse standpoints and looking at a situation or issue through the eyes of others can also be problematic for *presenters,* and they often fear opinions and points of view which diverge significantly from their own. They find criticism levelled at them by other people extremely hard to take, treating it as either an attack or a manifestation of spitefulness and, in general, they are incapable of putting it to constructive use. This works both ways, since they themselves find it equally difficult to express a critical opinion. When faced with problems, unpleasant situations or conflict, *presenters* tend to turn tail and run. As a rule, they do no better when it comes to routine tasks and repetitive activities and, in general, managing finances is not one of their strengths either.

Personal development

Presenters' personal development depends on the extent to which they make use of their natural potential and surmount the dangers inherent in their personality type. What follows are some practical tips which, together, form a specific guide that we might call *The Presenter's Ten Commandments*.

Keep your focus fixed

Determine your priorities and make a serious effort to finish what you undertake. Keep your eyes firmly fixed on the most crucial tasks and stop letting yourself be distracted by less important matters. Do that and you will find yourself avoiding frustration and achieving more.

Finish what you start

You launch into new things enthusiastically, but have problems with finishing what you have already begun – a *modus operandi* which usually produces mediocre results. Try sorting out what is most important to you and deciding how you want to accomplish it. Then knuckle down – and stick to the plan!

Stop being afraid of conflict

When you find yourself in a situation of conflict, stop hiding your head in the sand and, instead, voice your point of view and feelings openly. Conflict very often helps us to expose problems and solve them.

Keep your impulsiveness reigned in

Before you make a decision or commit yourself to something, devote a little time to gathering some relevant information, analysing it and evaluating the situation coolly and objectively. When you take that approach, you will most likely find yourself with less to do and, more to the point, you will end up doing it better.

Ask

Stop assuming that, if other people are silent, it means that they are indifferent or hostile. If you really want to know what they think, ask them.

Stop fearing criticism

Quell your fear of expressing your own critical opinions and of accepting criticism from others. Criticism can be constructive. There is no law which says that it has to mean attacking people or undermining their values.

Set yourself free from other people's opinions

You accept others, don't you? So start accepting yourself and stop evaluating yourself on the basis of what other people have to say about you. They could be wrong. They could even be lying. When it comes to making decisions about your life, who could possibly be more competent than you?

Avoid provisional solutions

When faced with difficulties, you have a tendency to act fast and go for solutions which are either provisional or simply defer the problem. Try looking at the wider picture and the long-term perspective instead. Devote some time to it and make it your aim not only to get rid of the issue itself, but also to solve it once and for all.

Stop fearing ideas and opinions which are different from yours

Before you reject them, give them some consideration and try to understand them. Being open to the viewpoints of others is not synonymous with discarding your own.

Start believing in a world which is more than just black and white

Try to look at problems in a wider context and from various angles. Things may be more complex than they seem to you. Your problems may not only be caused by others; they might also be caused by you! Remember, you may not always be in the right!

Well-known figures

Below is a list of some well-known people who match the *presenter's* profile:

- **Pablo Picasso** (1881-1973); a Spanish painter, sculptor, print artist and theatre designer, he pioneered the Cubist movement and is considered to be one of the most outstanding visual artists of the twentieth century.
- **Leonard Bernstein** (1918-1990); an American composer, pianist and conductor.
- **Gene Hackman** (born in 1930); an American screen actor, director and producer whose filmography includes *Crimson Tide*, he has won numerous prestigious awards.
- **Elvis Presley** (1935-1977); an American singer and screen actor, he was a precursor

of rock and roll and an icon of twentieth-century popular culture.

- **Al Pacino** (Alfred James Pacino; born in 1940); an American theatre and screen actor, filmmaker and screenwriter of Italian descent, his filmography includes *The Devil's Advocate*.

- **Joe Pesci** (Joseph Franco Pesci; born in 1943); an American screen actor whose filmography includes *Goodfellas*.

- **John Goodman** (born in 1952); an American film actor whose filmography includes *Blues Brothers*.

- **Branscombe Richmond** (born in 1955); an American screen actor whose filmography includes the *Renegade* TV series.

- **Linda Fiorentino** (born in 1958); an American screen actress whose filmography includes *Men in Black*.

- **Kevin Spacey** (Kevin Spacey Fowler; born in 1959); an American theatre and screen actor whose movies include *K-PAX*, he is also a director and producer.

- **Woody Harrelson** (born in 1961); an American screen actor whose filmography includes *Welcome to Sarajevo*.

- **Steve Irwin** (1962-2006); an Australian naturalist, television presenter and environmental activist.

- **Dean Cain** (Dean George Tanaka; born in 1966); an American film actor, producer, screenwriter and director whose filmography includes *Firetrap*.

- **Julie Bowen** (Julie Bowen Luetkemeyer; born in 1970); an American screen actress whose filmography includes *Venus and Mars*.
- **Josh Hartnett** (born in 1978); an American screen actor whose filmography includes *Black Hawk Down*.

The ID16™© Personality Types in a Nutshell

The Administrator (ESTJ)

Life motto: We'll get the job done!

Administrators are hard-working, responsible and extremely loyal. Energetic and decisive, they value order, stability, security and clear rules. They are matter-of-fact and businesslike, logical, rational and practical and possess the capability to assimilate large amounts of detailed information.

Superb organisers, they are intolerant of ineffectuality, wastefulness and slothfulness. True to their convictions and direct in their contact with others, they present their point of view decisively and openly express critical opinions, sometimes hurting other people as a result.

The *administrator*'s four natural inclinations:

- source of life energy: the exterior world
- mode of assimilating information: via the senses
- decision-making mode: the mind
- lifestyle: organised

Similar personality types:

- the Animator
- the Inspector
- the Practitioner

Statistical data:

- *administrators* constitute between ten and thirteen per cent of the global community
- men predominate among *administrators* (60 per cent)
- the United States is an example of a nation corresponding to the *administrator's* profile[3]

Find out more!

The Administrator. Your Guide to the ESTJ Personality Type by Jaroslaw Jankowski

---

[3] What this means is not that all the residents of the USA fall within this personality type, but that American society as a whole possesses a great many of the character traits typical of the *administrator.*

The Advocate (ESFJ)

Life motto: How can I help you?

Advocates are well-organised, energetic and enthusiastic. Practical, responsible and conscientious, they are sincere and exceptionally gregarious.

Advocates are perceptive of human feelings, emotions and needs. They value harmony and find criticism and conflict difficult to bear. With their sensitivity to any and every manifestation of injustice, prejudice or detriment to another, they are genuinely interested in other people's problems and take real delight in helping them and tending to their needs, while often neglecting their own. They have a tendency to do everything for others and can be vulnerable to manipulation.

The *advocate*'s four natural inclinations:

- source of life energy: the exterior world
- mode of assimilating information: via the senses
- decision-making mode: the heart
- lifestyle: organised

Similar personality types:

- the Presenter
- the Protector
- the Artist

Statistical data:

- *advocates* constitute between ten and thirteen per cent of the global community

- women predominate among *advocates* (70 per cent)
- Canada is an example of a nation corresponding to the *advocate's* profile

Find out more!

The Advocate. Your Guide to the ESFJ Personality Type by Jaroslaw Jankowski

The Animator (ESTP)

Life motto: Let's DO something!

Animators are energetic, active and enterprising. Fond of the company of others, they have the ability to enjoy the moment and are spontaneous, flexible and open to change.

Animators are inspirers and instigators, spurring others to act. Being logical, rational and pragmatic realists, they are wearied by abstract concepts and solutions for the future. Their focus is on solving concrete problems in the here and now. They have difficulties with organising and planning and can be impulsive, acting first and thinking later.

The *animator's* four natural inclinations:

- source of life energy: the exterior world
- mode of assimilating information: via the senses
- decision-making mode: the mind
- lifestyle: spontaneous

Similar personality types:

- the Administrator
- the Practitioner
- the Inspector

Statistical data:

- *animators* constitute between six and ten per cent of the global community
- men predominate among *animators* (60 per cent)
- Australia is an example of a nation corresponding to the *animator's* profile

Find out more!

The Animator. Your Guide to the ESTP Personality Type by Jaroslaw Jankowski

The Artist (ISFP)

Life motto: Let's create something!

Artists are sensitive, creative and original, with a sense of the aesthetic and natural artistic talents. Independent in character, they follow their own system of values and are optimistic in outlook, with a positive approach to life and an ability to enjoy the moment.

Helping others is a source of joy to them. They find abstract theories tedious and would rather create reality than talk about it, although starting on something new comes more easily to them than finishing what they have already started. They have difficulty in voicing their own desires and needs.

The *artist's* four natural inclinations:

- source of life energy: the interior world
- mode of assimilating information: via the senses
- decision-making mode: the heart
- lifestyle: spontaneous

Similar personality types:

- the Protector
- the Presenter
- the Advocate

Statistical data:

- *artists* constitute between six and nine per cent of the global community
- women predominate among *artists* (60 per cent)
- China is an example of a nation corresponding to the *artist's* profile

Find out more!

The Artist. Your Guide to the ISFP Personality Type by Jaroslaw Jankowski

The Counsellor (ENFJ)

Life motto: My friends are my world

Counsellors are optimistic, enthusiastic and quick-witted. Courteous and tactful, they have an extraordinary gift for empathy and find joy in acting for the good of others, with no thought of themselves. They have the ability to influence other people, inspiring them, eliciting their hidden potential and giving them faith in their own powers. Radiating warmth, they draw others to them and often help them in solving their personal problems.

Counsellors can be over-trusting and have a tendency to view the world through rose-tinted glasses. With their focus on other people, they often forget about their own needs.

The *counsellor's* four natural inclinations:

- source of life energy: the exterior world
- mode of assimilating information: intuition
- decision-making mode: the heart
- lifestyle: organised

Similar personality types:

- the Enthusiast
- the Mentor
- the Idealist

Statistical data:

- *counsellors* constitute between three and five per cent of the global community
- women predominate among *counsellors* (80 per cent)
- France is an example of a nation corresponding to the *counsellor's* profile

Find out more!

The Counsellor. Your Guide to the ENFJ Personality Type by Jaroslaw Jankowski

The Director (ENTJ)

Life motto: I'll tell you what you need to do.

Directors are independent, active and decisive. Rational, logical and creative, when they analyse problems they look at the wider picture and are able to foresee the future consequences of human activities. They are characterised by optimism and a healthy sense of their own worth and are capable of transforming theoretical concepts into concrete, practical plans of action.

Visionaries, mentors and organisers, *directors* possess natural leadership skills. Their powerful personalities and direct and critical style can often have an intimidating effect, causing them problems in their interpersonal relationships.

The *director's* four natural inclinations:

- source of life energy: the exterior world
- mode of assimilating information: intuition
- decision-making mode: the mind
- lifestyle: organised

Similar personality types:

- the Innovator
- the Strategist
- the Logician

Statistical data:

- *directors* constitute between two and five per cent of the global community
- men predominate among *directors* (70 per cent)

- Holland is an example of a nation corresponding to the *director's* profile

Find out more!

The Director. Your Guide to the ENTJ Personality Type by Jaroslaw Jankowski

The Enthusiast (ENFP)

Life motto: We'll manage!

Enthusiasts are energetic, enthusiastic and optimistic. Capable of enjoying life and looking ahead to the future, they are dynamic, quick-witted and creative. They have a liking for people in general, value honest and genuine relationships and are warm, sincere and emotional. Criticism is something they handle badly. With their gift for empathy and ability to perceive people's needs, feelings and motives, they both inspire others and infect them with their own enthusiasm.

They love to be at the centre of events and are flexible and capable of improvising. Their inclination leads towards idealistic notions. Being easily distracted, they have problems with seeing things through to the end.

The *enthusiast's* four natural inclinations:

- source of life energy: the exterior world
- mode of assimilating information: intuition
- decision-making mode: the heart
- lifestyle: spontaneous

Similar personality types:

- the Counsellor
- the Idealist
- the Mentor

Statistical data:

- *enthusiasts* constitute between five and eight per cent of the global community
- women predominate among *enthusiasts* (60 per cent)
- Italy is an example of a nation corresponding to the *enthusiast's* profile

Find out more!

The Enthusiast. Your Guide to the ENFP Personality Type by Jaroslaw Jankowski

The Idealist (INFP)

Life motto: We CAN live differently.

Idealists are sensitive, loyal, and creative. Living in accordance with the values they hold is of immense importance to them and they both manifest an interest in the reality of the spirit and delve deeply into the mysteries of life. Wrapped up in the world's problems and open to the needs of other people, they prize harmony and balance.

Idealists are romantic; not only are they able to show love, but they also need warmth and affection themselves. With their outstanding ability to read other people's feelings and emotions, they build healthy, profound and enduring relationships. They feel that they are on very shaky ground in situations of conflict and have no real resistance to stress and criticism.

The *idealist's* four natural inclinations:

- source of life energy: the interior world
- mode of assimilating information: intuition
- decision-making mode: the heart
- lifestyle: spontaneous

Similar personality types:

- the Mentor
- the Enthusiast
- the Counsellor

Statistical data:

- *idealists* constitute between one and four per cent of the global community
- women predominate among *idealists* (60 per cent)
- Thailand is an example of a nation corresponding to the *idealist's* profile

Find out more!

The Idealist. Your Guide to the INFP Personality Type by Jaroslaw Jankowski

The Innovator (ENTP)

Life motto: How about trying a different approach…?

Innovators are inventive, original and independent. Optimistic, energetic and enterprising, they are people of action who love being at the centre of events and solving 'insoluble' problems. Their thoughts are turned to the future and they are curious about the world and visionary by nature. Open to new concepts and ideas, they enjoy new experiences and experiments and have the ability to identify the connections between separate events.

Innovators are spontaneous, communicative and self-assured. However, they tend to overestimate their own possibilities and have problems with seeing things through to the end. They are also inclined to be impatient and to take risks.

The *innovator's* four natural inclinations:

- source of life energy: the exterior world
- mode of assimilating information: intuition
- decision-making mode: the mind
- lifestyle: spontaneous

Similar personality types:

- the Director
- the Logician
- the Strategist

Statistical data:

- *innovators* constitute between three and five per cent of the global community

- men predominate among *innovators* (70 per cent)
- Israel is an example of a nation corresponding to the *innovator's* profile

Find out more!

The Innovator. Your Guide to the ENTP Personality Type by Jaroslaw Jankowski

The Inspector (ISTJ)

Life motto: *Duty first.*

Inspectors are people who can always be counted on. Well-mannered, punctual, reliable, conscientious and responsible, when they give their word, they keep it. Being analytical, methodical, systematic and logical by nature, they tend be seen as serious, cold and reserved. They prize calm, stability and order, have no fondness for change and like clear principles and concrete rules.

Inspectors are hard-working, persevering and capable of seeing things through to the end. As perfectionists, they try to exercise control over everything within their sphere and are sparing in their praise. They also underrate the importance of other people's feelings and emotions.

The *inspector's* four natural inclinations:

- source of life energy: the interior world
- mode of assimilating information: via the senses

- decision-making mode: the mind
- lifestyle: organised

Similar personality types:

- the Practitioner
- the Administrator
- the Animator

Statistical data:

- *inspectors* constitute between six and ten per cent of the global community
- men predominate among *inspectors* (60 per cent)
- Switzerland is an example of a nation corresponding to the *inspector's* profile

Find out more!

The Inspector. Your Guide to the ISTJ Personality Type by Jaroslaw Jankowski

The Logician (INTP)

Life motto: Above all else, seek to discover the truths about the world.

Logicians are original, resourceful and creative. With a love for solving problems of a theoretical nature, they are analytical, quick-witted, enthusiastically disposed towards new concepts and have the ability to connect individual phenomena, educing general rules and theories from them. Logical, exact and inquiring, they are quick to spot incoherence and inconsistency.

Logicians are independent, sceptical of existing solutions and authorities, tolerant and open to new challenges. When immersed in thought, they will sometimes lose touch with the outside world.

The *logician's* four natural inclinations:

- source of life energy: the interior world
- mode of assimilating information: intuition
- decision-making mode: the mind
- lifestyle: spontaneous

Similar personality types:

- the Strategist
- the Innovator
- the Director

Statistical data:

- *logicians* constitute between two and three per cent of the global community;
- men predominate among *logicians* (80 per cent)
- India is an example of a nation corresponding to the *logician's* profile

Find out more!

The Logician. Your Guide to the INTP Personality Type by Jaroslaw Jankowski

The Mentor (INFJ)

Life motto: The world CAN be a better place!

Mentors are creative and sensitive. With their gaze fixed firmly on the future, they spot opportunities and potential imperceptible to others. Idealists and visionaries, they are geared towards helping people and are conscientious, responsible and, at one and the same time, courteous, caring and friendly. They strive to understand the mechanisms governing the world and view problems from a wide perspective.

Superb listeners and observers, *mentors* are characterised by their extraordinary empathy, intuition and trust of people and are capable of reading the feelings and emotions of others. They find criticism and conflict difficult to bear and can come across as enigmatic.

The *mentor's* four natural inclinations:

- source of life energy: the interior world
- mode of assimilating information: intuition
- decision-making mode: the heart
- lifestyle: organised

Similar personality types:

- the Idealist
- the Counsellor
- the Enthusiast

Statistical data:

- *mentors* constitute one per cent of the global community and are the most rarely occurring of the sixteen personality types

- women predominate among *mentors* (80 per cent)
- Norway is an example of a nation corresponding to the *mentor's* profile

Find out more!

The Mentor. Your Guide to the INFJ Personality Type
by Jaroslaw Jankowski

The Practitioner (ISTP)

Life motto: Actions speak louder than words.

Practitioners are optimistic and spontaneous, with a positive approach to life. Reserved and independent, they hold true to their personal convictions and view external principles and norms with scepticism. They find abstract concepts and solutions for the future tiresome and would far rather roll up their sleeves and get to work on solving tangible and concrete problems.

Adapting well to new places and situations, they enjoy fresh challenges and risks and are capable of keeping a cool head in the face of threats and danger. Their general reticence and extreme reserve when it comes to expressing their opinions mean that other people may often find them impenetrable.

The *practitioner's* four natural inclinations:

- source of life energy: the interior world
- mode of assimilating information: via the senses

- decision-making mode: the mind
- lifestyle: spontaneous

Similar personality types:

- the Inspector
- the Animator
- the Administrator

Statistical data:

- *practitioners* constitute between six and nine per cent of the global community
- men predominate among *practitioners* (60 per cent)
- Singapore is an example of a nation corresponding to the *practitioner's* profile

Find out more!

The Practitioner. Your Guide to the ISTP Personality Type by Jaroslaw Jankowski

The Presenter (ESFP)

Life motto: Now is the perfect moment!

Presenters are optimistic, energetic and outgoing, with the ability to enjoy life and have fun to the full. Practical, flexible and spontaneous at one and the same time, they enjoy change and new experiences, coping badly with solitude, stagnation and routine.

With their liking for being at the centre of attention, they are natural-born actors and their speaking abilities arouse the interest and enthusiasm of their listeners. Focused as they are on the present moment, they will sometimes lose sight of their long-term aims and can also have problems with foreseeing the consequences of their actions.

The *presenter's* four natural inclinations:

- source of life energy: the exterior world
- mode of assimilating information: via the senses
- decision-making mode: the heart
- lifestyle: spontaneous

Similar personality types:

- the Advocate
- the Artist
- the Protector

Statistical data:

- *presenters* constitute between eight and thirteen per cent of the global community
- women predominate among *presenters* (60 per cent)
- Brazil is an example of a nation corresponding to the *presenter's* profile

Find out more!

The Presenter. Your Guide to the ESFP Personality Type by Jaroslaw Jankowski

The Protector (ISFJ)

Life motto: Your happiness matters to me.

Protectors are sincere, warm-hearted, unassuming, trustworthy and extraordinarily loyal. With their ability to perceive people's needs and their desire to help them, they will always put others first. Practical, well-organised and gifted with both an eye and a memory for detail, they are responsible, hard-working, patient, persevering and capable of seeing things through to the end.

Protectors set great store by tranquillity, stability and friendly relations with others and are skilled at building bridges between people. By the same token, they find conflict and criticism difficult to bear. Given their powerful sense of duty and their constant readiness to come to the aid of others, they can end up being used by people.

The *protector's* four natural inclinations:

- source of life energy: the interior world
- mode of assimilating information: via the senses
- decision-making mode: the heart
- lifestyle: organised

Similar personality types:

- the Artist
- the Advocate
- the Presenter

Statistical data:

- *protectors* constitute between eight and twelve per cent of the global population
- women predominate among *protectors* (70 per cent)
- Sweden is an example of a nation corresponding to the *protector's* profile

Find out more!

The Protector. Your Guide to the ISFJ Personality Type by Jaroslaw Jankowski

The Strategist (INTJ)

Life motto: I can certainly improve this.

Strategists are independent and outstandingly individualistic, with an immense seam of inner energy. Creative, inventive and resourceful, others perceive them as competent, self-assured and, at one and the same time, distant and enigmatic. No matter what they turn their attention to, they will always look at the bigger picture and they have a driving urge to improve the world around them and set it in order.

Well-organised, responsible, critical and demanding, they are difficult to knock off balance – and just as hard to please to the full. Reading the emotions and feelings of others is something they find very problematic.

The *strategist's* four natural inclinations:

- source of life energy: the interior world

- mode of assimilating information: intuition
- decision-making mode: the mind
- lifestyle: organised

Similar personality types:

- the Logician
- the Director
- the Innovator

Statistical data:

- *strategists* constitute between one and two per cent of the global community
- men predominate among *strategists* (80 per cent)
- Finland is an example of a nation corresponding to the *strategist's* profile

Find out more!

The Strategist. Your Guide to the INTJ Personality Type by Jaroslaw Jankowski

Additional information

The four natural inclinations

1. THE DOMINANT SOURCE OF LIFE ENERGY

   a. THE EXTERIOR WORLD
   People who draw their energy from outside. They need activity and contact with others and find being alone for any length of time hard to bear.

   b. THE INTERIOR WORLD
   People who draw their energy from their inner world. They need quiet and solitude and feel drained when they spend any length of time in a group.

2. THE DOMINANT MODE OF ASSIMILATING INFORMATION

a. VIA THE SENSES
People who rely on the five senses and are persuaded by facts and evidence. They have a liking for methods and practices which are tried and tested and prefer concrete tasks and are realists who trust in experience.

b. VIA INTUITION
People who rely on the sixth sense and are driven by what they 'feel in their bones'. They have a liking for innovative solutions and problems of a theoretical nature and are characterised by a creative approach to their tasks and the ability to predict.

3. THE DOMINANT DECISION-MAKING MODE

a. THE MIND
People who are guided by logic and objective principles. They are critical and direct in expressing their opinions.

b. THE HEART
People who are guided by their feelings and values. They long for harmony and mutual understanding with others.

4. THE DOMINANT LIFESTYLE

a. ORGANISED
People who are conscientious and organised. They value order and like to operate according to plan.

b. SPONTANEOUS
People who are spontaneous and value freedom of action. They live for the moment and have no trouble finding their feet in new situations.

The approximate percentage of each personality type in the world population

Personality Type:	Proportion:
• The Administrator (ESTJ):	10-13%
• The Advocate (ESFJ):	10-13%
• The Animator (ESTP):	6-10%
• The Artist (ISFP):	6-9%
• The Counsellor (ENFJ):	3-5 %
• The Director (ENTJ):	2-5%
• The Enthusiast (ENFP):	5-8%
• The Idealist (INFP):	1-4%
• The Innovator (ENTP):	3-5%
• The Inspector (ISTJ):	6-10%
• The Logician (INTP):	2-3%
• The Mentor (INFJ):	ca. 1%
• The Practitioner (ISTP):	6-9%
• The Presenter (ESFP):	8-13%

- The Protector (ISFJ):   8-12%
- The Strategist (INTJ):   1-2%

The approximate percentage of women and men of each personality type in the world population

Personality Type:	Women / Men:
The Administrator (ESTJ):	40% / 60%
The Advocate (ESFJ):	70% / 30%
The Animator (ESTP):	40% / 60%
The Artist (ISFP):	60% / 40%
The Counsellor (ENFJ):	80% / 20%
The Director (ENTJ):	30% / 70%
The Enthusiast (ENFP):	60% / 40%
The Idealist (INFP):	60% / 40%
The Innovator (ENTP):	30% / 70%
The Inspector (ISTJ):	40% / 60%
The Logician (INTP):	20% / 80%
The Mentor (INFJ):	80% / 20%
The Practitioner (ISTP):	40% / 60%
The Presenter (ESFP):	60% / 40%
The Protector (ISFJ):	70% / 30%
The Strategist (INTJ):	20% / 80%

Bibliography

- Arraj, Tyra & Arraj, James: *Tracking the Elusive Human, Volume 1: A Practical Guide to C.G. Jung's Psychological Types, W.H. Sheldon's Body and Temperament Types and Their Integration*, Inner Growth Books, 1988

- Arraj, James: *Tracking the Elusive Human, Volume 2: An Advanced Guide to the Typological Worlds of C. G. Jung, W.H. Sheldon, Their Integration, and the Biochemical Typology of the Future*, Inner Growth Books, 1990

- Berens, Linda V.; Cooper, Sue A.; Ernst, Linda K.; Martin, Charles R.; Myers, Steve; Nardi, Dario; Pearman, Roger R.; Segal, Marci; Smith, Melissa: *A Quick Guide to the 16 Personality Types in Organizations: Understanding Personality Differences in the Workplace*, Telos Publications, 2002

- Geier, John G. & Downey, E. Dorothy: *Energetics of Personality*, Aristos Publishing House, 1989

- Hunsaker, Phillip L. & Alessandra, Anthony J.: *The Art of Managing People*, Simon and Schuster, 1986

- Jung, Carl Gustav: *Psychological Types (The Collected Works of C. G. Jung, Vol. 6)*, Princeton University Press, 1976

- Kise, Jane A. G.; Stark, David & Krebs Hirsch, Sandra: *Lifekeys: Discover Who You Are*, Bethany House, 2005
- Kroeger, Otto & Thuesen, Janet: *Type Talk or How to Determine Your Personality Type and Change Your Life*, Delacorte Press, 1988
- Lawrence, Gordon: *People Types and Tiger Stripes*, Center for Applications of Psychological Type, 1993
- Lawrence, Gordon: *Looking at Type and Learning Styles*, Center for Applications of Psychological Type, 1997
- Maddi, Salvatore R.: *Personality Theories: A Comparative Analysis*, Waveland, 2001
- Martin, Charles R.: *Looking at Type: The Fundamentals Using Psychological Type To Understand and Appreciate Ourselves and Others*, Center for Applications of Psychological Type, 2001
- Meier C.A.: Personality: *The Individuation Process in the Light of C. G. Jung's Typology*, Daimon Verlag, 2007
- Pearman, Roger R. & Albritton, Sarah: *I'm Not Crazy, I'm Just Not You: The Real Meaning of the Sixteen Personality Types*, Davies-Black Publishing, 1997
- Segal, Marci: Creativity and Personality Type: *Tools for Understanding and Inspiring the Many Voices of Creativity*, Telos Publications, 2001
- Sharp, Daryl: Personality Type: *Jung's Model of Typology*, Inner City Books, 1987
- Spoto, Angelo: *Jung's Typology in Perspective*, Chiron Publications, 1995
- Tannen, Deborah: *You Just Don't Understand*, William Morrow and Company, 1990
- Thomas, Jay C. & Segal, Daniel L.: *Comprehensive Handbook of Personality and Psychopathology, Personality and Everyday Functioning*, Wiley, 2005
- Thomson, Lenore: *Personality Type: An Owner's Manual*, Shambhala, 1998
- Tieger, Paul D. & Barron-Tieger Barbara: *Just Your Type: Create the Relationship You've Always Wanted Using the Secrets of Personality Type*, Little, Brown and Company, 2000
- Von Franz, Marie-Louise & Hillman, James: *Lectures on Jung's Typology*, Continuum International Publishing Group, 1971

www.ingramcontent.com/pod-product-compliance
Lightning Source LLC
Chambersburg PA
CBHW031209020426
42333CB00013B/854